Festival in My Heart
Poems by Japanese Children

Festival in My Heart
Poems by Japanese Children

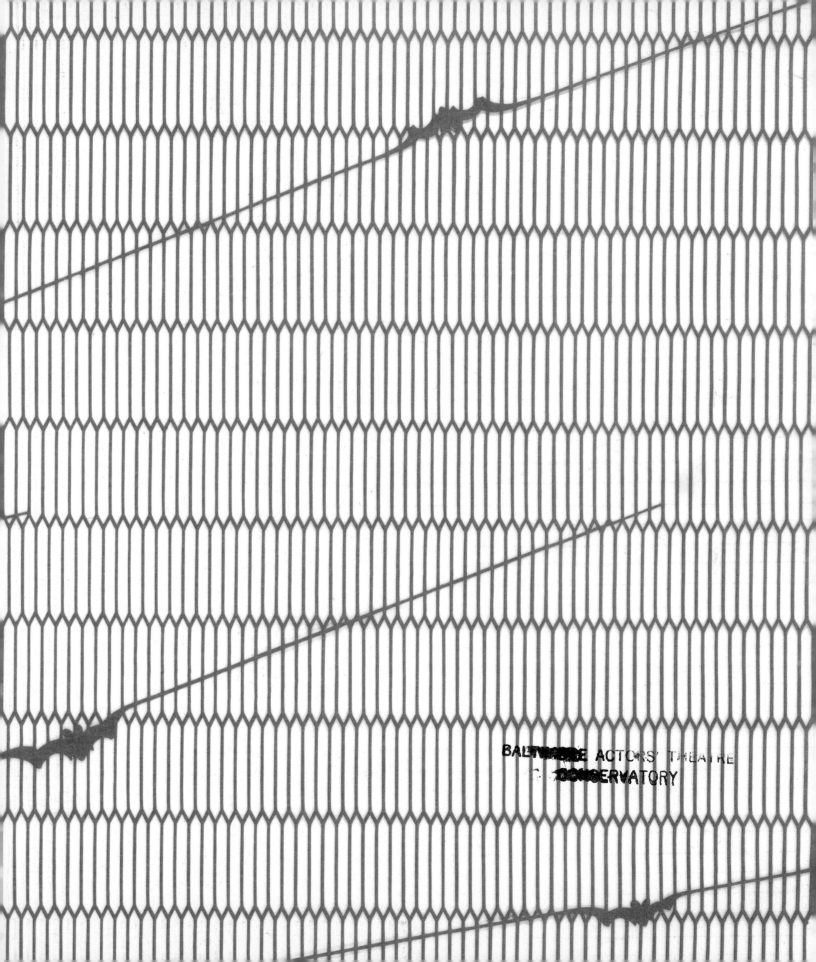

Selected and translated from the Japanese
by Bruno Navasky
Harry N. Abrams, Inc., Publishers

TO MY PARENTS, WITH LOVE AND WONDER

Editor: ELLEN ROSEFSKY
Designer: DARILYN LOWE CARNES
Photo Research: NEIL RYDER HOOS

Library of Congress Cataloging-in-Publication Data
Festival in my heart: poems by Japanese children/selected and
    translated by Bruno Navasky.
        p. cm.
    Includes index.
    Summary: An illustrated collection of poetry written by Japanese
elementary school children that provides a portrait of an often
mysterious and elusive culture.
    ISBN 0–8109–3314–4
    1. Children's poetry, Japanese—Translations into English.
    2. School verse, Japanese—Translations into English.   3. Children's
writings, Japanese—Translations into English.   4. Art, Japanese.
[1. Japanese poetry—Collections.   2. Children's writings.]
I. Navasky, Bruno Peter, 1967–
PL757.4.C45F47 1993
895.6'150809282—dc20   93–18251
                                                             CIP
                                                             AC

Endpapers: UNKNOWN. *Bat Motif on Honeycombed Ground* (stencil). Edo period, late 19th century. Paper and silk thread, 17⅜×17⅜″. The Art Institute of Chicago. Gift of G. H. Saddard

Pages 2–3: TOSA MITSUOKI. *Maple Leaves with Poem Slips.* Edo period, c. 1644–78. Six-fold screen: Ink, colors, gold leaf, and powdered gold on silk, 56⅛×115½″. The Art Institute of Chicago; Kate S. Buckingham Fund

Editor's note: Every attempt was made to obtain permission for all of the contributor's poems in this book.

Copyright © 1993 Harry N. Abrams, Inc.

Published in 1993 by Harry N. Abrams, Incorporated, New York
A Times Mirror Company

Printed and bound in Japan

SESSHU TOYO. *Mountain Landscape.*
15th–16th century. Painting, 6⅜ × 13⅞".
Courtesy of the Freer Gallery of Art,
Smithsonian Institution, Washington,
D.C.

PREFACE
By Kawasaki Hiroshi

T HE POEMS collected here were originally published in the "Lifestyle & Culture" section of a Japanese newspaper called the *Yomiuri Shimbun*. Among these poems are the words of children too young to write, copied down and sent in by family members (usually the mothers). Since the inception of the "Poems by Children" column in 1982, it has been my constant pleasure to read the submitted poems, make selections, and accompany them with my own brief written impressions. I write poetry myself, but, reading these poems by children, I often have a feeling of renewal—as if all my senses have been made new, as if some rust has dropped from them.

It goes without saying that young people know fewer words than adults. But still they write poems that strike to the quick of our hearts. There are times when these poems appeal because the children are making do with words at hand to express what they want, and this echoes all the more freshly in our grown-up ears. But there are also instances when the poems themselves are wonderful simply as poems.

On the island of Okinawa there is a saying, "Wisdom from children." By "wisdom" they don't mean that children have knowledge or access to information, but rather that children are innocent, pure of heart, and, thus, they see the very essence of things: their senses attain to the worlds of the spirit and of the supernatural. When I read the poems, I am often struck by the thought that they demonstrate the truth of this proverb: children often seem to find life in inorganic objects, and this is evident in their poems. In Japan, in our earliest history, there were many who believed that gods and spirits dwelt in trees, light, land, even rocks, and who would listen to the voices therein and make offerings. And now in the present, there are children still who have soul enough to greet the natural world as a friend, innocently—I believe these are the ones who will write poems to make us adults gasp with wonder. These are things only children can put into words simply because they are children, the way a blind person sometimes may see things that sighted people cannot.

The abundance of children's powers of imagination is truly terrifying. What is in a child's head while walking down the road or strolling down a path? The child might be just then riding on the back of a dreamworld elephant, or listening to the sound of a dinosaur's egg cracking. We have all experienced moments such as these when we were young. And there are times when children's poems play the voices of angels, moments when they offer the keenest cultural criticism. The life of the child, one that can breathe back into us the abilities and senses we lost in growing up, is a life worthy of our highest respect.

That these poems are now being translated into English, and that they will be read for the first time by people overseas, pleases me through and through. I offer thanks to the translator, Bruno Navasky, and to everyone involved in the publication of this book.

UNKNOWN. *Butterflies and Plants on Vertically Striped Ground* (stencil). Edo period, late 19th century. Paper and silk thread, 13 × 16⅝″. The Art Institute of Chicago. Frederick W. Gookin Collection

The Ages Flow

The old brown photo album.
Grandfather's pictures tell of
Meiji, Taishō, Shōwa—
all the ages slowly
flowing by.
Smelling a little moldy,
the black-and-white photos
tell sturdily a tale of history.

Ikenaga Eri, fifth grade

My Family

I was born
in the year of the rooster
so I wake up early.
My brother was born
in the year of the monkey
so he likes to climb trees.
My father was born
in the year of the dragon
so he likes to eat spicy food
and breathe fire.
My mother was born
in the year of the sheep—
but she doesn't really
seem like one.

Ueda Akie, third grade

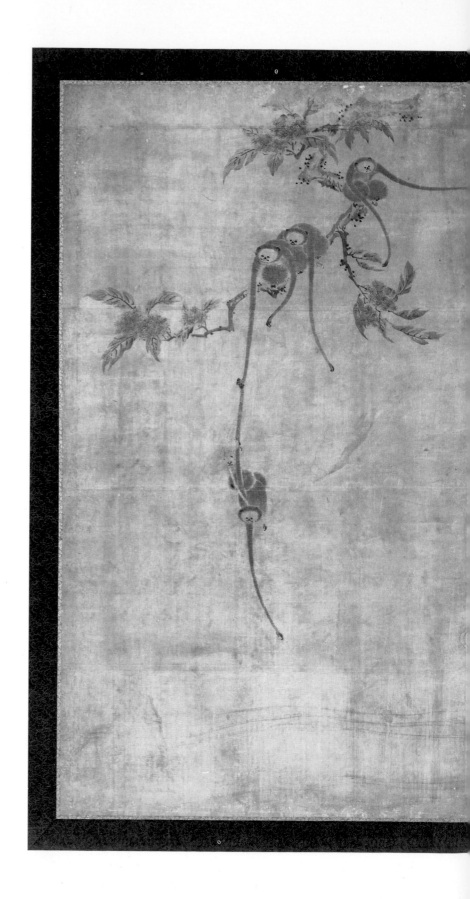

ANONYMOUS. *Gibbons*. 17th century.
Two-panel screen: ink on paper,
68½ × 74¼". Los Angeles County
Museum of Art. Etsuko and Joe Price
Collection

My Brother

They were teasing my older brother.
I cried and ran back in the house.
"It's not fair," I was thinking
and covering my face with my hands.
When I breathed *whoo* it was a cool breath
and when I breathed *hah* hot breath
came out.
Breathing *hah*, that's like my brother.

Ogura Mitsuru, second grade

9

Baby Room

In the baby room
in mommy's belly
there are
three beds.
My brother Shii
got up first
then came the next one
and I
overslept.

Doi Takashi, kindergarten

Open

I open my eyes.
I open the curtains.
I open my mouth to say "good morning."
At breakfast time
I open the refrigerator.
"I'm going out" I say,
and open the door.
Like opening a new book,
one day starts.

Chikaoka Saori, fourth grade

Mom

Hey mom—
Do you know why I was born?
I wanted to meet you, mom,
so I got born.

Tanaka Daisuke, kindergarten

UNKNOWN. *Anesama ningyō* (Elder-Sister dolls). Late Meiji, early Taishō period. Paper, corn husk, cloth, clay, applied color, 4½" to 12¼". Collection Honolulu Academy of Arts, Frederick Starr Collection, Gift of Ruth Knudsen Hanner, 1951

opposite:
UNKNOWN. *Chigo Daishi*. Late 13th century. Hanging scroll: color on silk, 18×15". Collection Kōsetsu Art Museum

Man and Woman Dancing (Haniwa found at Kōnan-mura, Saitama Pref.). 6th–7th century. Clay figures, 25⅛″ and 22¼″. Tokyo National Museum

Ancestors

Papa was born from my grandmother in Shichiri.
My Shichiri grandmother
was born from a grandmother
way out in the country.
I think the country grandmother
was born from another grandmother
way way out in the country.
It goes all the way back—just women.

Kabe Yasuko, kindergarten

RYUKOSAI. *The Actor Tamejuro Holding up a Dancing Puppet*. Late 18th century. Woodblock print, 11½ × 5½″. Courtesy of The Art Institute of Chicago. Frederick W. Gookin Collection

When I Get Big

When I get big,
I want to be a pickled plum
and I want mom to be a *shiso* leaf
so that we'll be always together.

Sekimoto Ayaka, kindergarten

My Brother's Eyes

My little brother is laughing
while he drinks barley tea.
I can't see his mouth
but I can tell from his eyes—
naughty eyes.
This time
they're thinking,
what'll I do next?

Takahashi Eriko, fourth grade

Children's Day

We went to a beauty salon
and they made me pretty
like a bride.
My friend Megumi also came.
Going down the stairs afterward,
suddenly I thought I might fall.
We got in the car to the shrine
and when we got our blessing
my leg fell asleep.
They gave us coloring books, pencils,
and thousand-year sweets.
We walked slowly,
holding the ends of our *kimono*.

Sekine Yachiyo, first grade

CHOBUNSAI EISHI. *Two Young Women Walking Through the Fields Accompanied by a Young Girl Carrying a Closed Umbrella*. c. 1788. Print, 14⅝ × 9⅞". The Metropolitan Museum of Art, New York. The Henry L. Phillips Collection, Bequest of Henry L. Phillips, 1940

Maze

Western clothes
are like a maze.
Because you never know
where your hands should go.

Noda Kōhei, kindergarten

Marriage

I'm marrying Masashi—
because I like him.
Ryoko is marrying Yū.
The girls
all know who
but the boys
don't know at all.

Tezuka Maiko, kindergarten

Dream

I had a dream
that a ghost appeared
and ate me up.
But then
my sister
ate the ghost.
My sister
is incredible.

KATSUSHIKA HOKUSAI. *The Ghost of Kohada Koheiji*. From *One Hundred Tales*. Edo period, c. 1831. Multicolor woodblock print, Chūban. Tokyo National Museum

Shimaoka Kōtarō, first grade

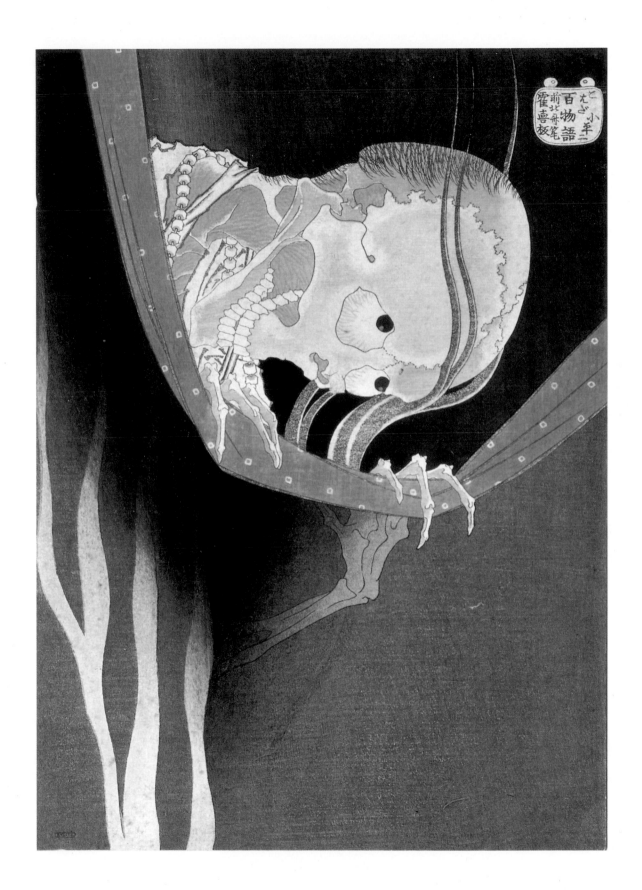

In the Sun

I think grandpa is in the sun
because he died in a fire.
The sun looks like a fire to me.
"Grandpa come and play" I say
but he's already gone.

Sakakibara Takashi, kindergarten

One Photo

There are lots of chrysanthemums
and the smell of incense
is drifting up.
On the coffin lie
the thousand paper cranes we folded.
Here and there,
the sound of sniffling.
In the middle of that,
one person's
laughing photo.

Matsuki Wataru, seventh grade

UNKNOWN. *The Priest Shunjōbō Chōgen*.
Early 13th century. Wood with paint,
32⅜" high. Tōdaiji, Nara

19

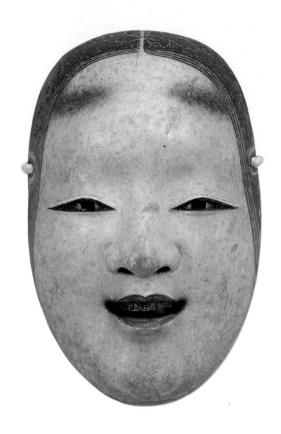

Noh Mask of Young Woman. Momoyama period. Carved wood with paint, 8³/₈ × 5³/₈″. Tokyo National Museum

Grandma's Wrinkles

My grandmother's face
is covered with wrinkles.
If you count on her forehead
there are twelve big ones.
I drew a picture
of grandma's face—
I only drew a few wrinkles,
little ones so grandma
was very happy
and laughed. Then
there were more wrinkles than before,
but I didn't tell her so.

Ishii Satoshi, kindergarten

Grandma's Sumō

My grandmother was watching *sumō*
on television.
She shouted
"Go Terao! Don't let Konishiki win!"
When Terao lost, she said
"He lost to the Hawaiian . . ."
I said "Grandma,
that's discrimination!"
and she said
"Don't you feel sorry
for the little Japanese?"
But except for *sumō*
she doesn't discriminate.

Usui Satoru, fifth grade

Ring-Entering Ceremony

Pachin!
Shuri-shuri.
Pachin!
Pakah!
Shoo . . .
Dosun!
Kyuu-kyuu-kyuu.
Shoo . . .
Dosun!
Kyuu-kyuu-kyuu.
Shoo . . . shoo . . .
The *yokozuna** enters the ring.

Tamura Rui, second grade

*A *sumō* wrestler of the highest rank

Sumo Wrestler Kite. From *The Art of the Japanese Kite* by Tal Streeter, Weatherhill Publishers, 1974

Cat

The cat
glowers
at me.
I got scared.
But the cat
also got scared.

Nomura Yuka, third grade

SOGA SHOHAKU. *Tiger*. Edo period, mid-
18th century. Hanging scroll: ink on
paper, 52½×21⅛". Courtesy, Museum
of Fine Arts, Boston. William Sturgis
Bigelow Collection

安永巳疢仲夏寫

應擧

MARUYAMA ŌKYO. *Puppies Gamboling in the Snow*. 18th century. Hanging scroll, 15½ × 20¾″. The Minneapolis Institute of Arts

Dog Training

The dog
was barking—
bow wow!
The lady said
"Quiet!"
very loudly but
he didn't stop so
she hit him.
Just like a dog owner,
I thought.
That was really hard.
Everyone at home said
"If he doesn't cry,
then he won't learn."
Just as if
they were talking about me.

Wakamatsu Shigeo, fifth grade

23

The Sun

Mother hung the *futon* out
and in the evening
she took it down.
I smelled the *futon* smell.
It was a good smell.
I said to mother
"The sun
is friendly, isn't it?"
and mother said
"It's true."
It is true that the sun is friendly.

Takeda Aiko, fourth grade

New Folk Tale

A long time ago, far away,
there once lived
an old man and an old woman.
The old woman was doing her wash
in the laundry machine
and a big peach came floating out.
Yes,
and then the washing machine said
*Fuzzy!**

Kunii Keisuke, kindergarten

* Japanese washing machines are often labeled "fuzzy," after their
  programmable "fuzzy logic" circuits.

Washing Machine

The washing machine
looks happy
when mommy
gets in the bath—
it spins round and round.

Tajima Naoto, kindergarten

GENKI. *Woman Under a Willow*. Mid-
18th century. Ink and color on silk,
40³/₁₆ × 14½". The Gitter Collection

Bath and Hair

When you get out of the bath
steam comes off your hair.
Maybe all the lies you tell
and the bad things you do
in one day
dissolve in the bath
and that's why
your hair steams.

Nishimura Tamiko, second grade

Working Mother

We're going to eat
at the *sushi* shop where mother works.
Even when we come
mother treats us
like customers.
Mother's work
is to carry things.
I get tired just watching.
I watch mother's sweat.
She wipes it with her arm
while she works.

Michinishi Kiyohiko, fifth grade

KITAGAWA UTAMARO. *A Mother Bathing Her Son*. Late 18th century. Color woodblock print, 14⅞ × 10⅛". The Nelson-Atkins Museum of Art, Kansas City, Missouri; Nelson Fund

Shedding

Mother takes a razor
and shaves her eyebrow hairs
and shaves under her nose—
she does it fast.
She rubs white stuff
on her face so everywhere
except her eyes and mouth
turns white like a ghost.
When she rubs off
the beauty cream
in little white flakes
it looks just like
she's shedding her skin.

Uto Izumu, first grade

KITAGAWA UTAMARO. *Model Patterns for Diaphanous Fabric*. c. 1795. Color woodblock print with dark mica background, 38¼×9½". Courtesy Musées Royaux d'Art et d'Histoire, Brussels

opposite:
FOUKOUSA. *Japanese Textile*. End of 19th century. Textile, 29⅞×27½". Musée des Arts Decoratifs, Paris

Dinner Table

The tofu
is taking a bath.
The fish
gets in bed.
The soy sauce
stays up late.

Tani Kaori, kindergarten

ATTRIBUTED TO FUJIWARA NOBUZANE.
Portrait of Minamoto no Kintada. 13th
century. Hanging scroll: ink and color on
paper, 11¹⁵⁄₁₆ × 20¼″ (overall). Courtesy of
the Freer Galley of Art, Smithsonian
Institution, Washington, D.C.

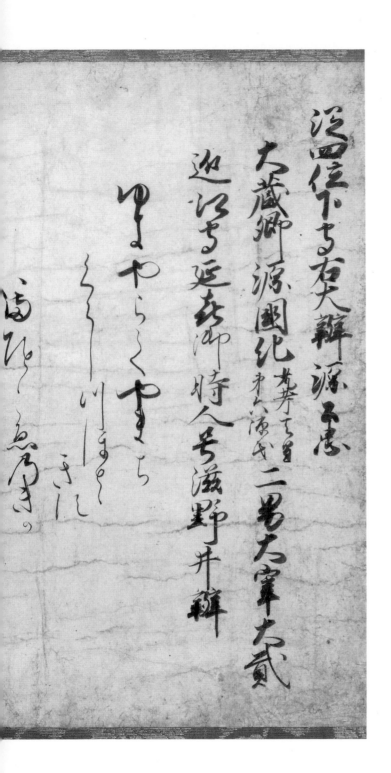

His Majesty the Emperor

When His Majesty the Emperor
takes one step,
cameras click
and people come running.
If I take one step,
nobody looks
or takes pictures.
It's a little lonely,
but—
I have freedom.

Arai Tsuyoshi, third grade

31

Father and Mother

I like my father
and my mother.
Father brings his salary home
and then mother
says "You work so hard! Thank you."
Father and mother
really do
get along well.

Tachimura Hiroyuki, second grade

Labor Day

Mommy left.
She left the cleaning
the laundry
the cooking
all to me
and shouldered her happiness
and turned to the airport
and went away to her
four days of Labor Day.
I hope it's sunny in Okinawa.

Katō Akemi, sixth grade

MASSHIRO. *One Hundred Women*. n.d.
Hanging scroll: color on silk, 44¾ ×
16⁹⁄₁₆". Los Angeles County Museum of
Art. Etsuko and Joe Price Collection

老豐千抱虎睡拾得
寒山打作一團做場大
夢當風流依二老樹
寒巖底

祥寿紹密拜手

The Watch

A watch
is always, always moving.
When you listen close
it's talking—
"I'm tired."
There are lots of different watches.
All of them
are talking—
"We're tired."

Higuchi Tomoko, first grade

MOKUAN REIEN. *The Four Sleepers*. 14th
century. Hanging scroll: brush on paper,
29 × 12¹³⁄₁₆″. Maeda Ikutoku-kai
Foundation, Tokyo

What Daddy Likes

Daddy likes
to sing
karaoké songs.
He sings and he sweats
and I try to make him laugh
by doing a funny dance
next to him while he's singing.
My father
sings well,
even while laughing.

Inazawa Miyako, second grade

To Father

Ohh, he left.
"Bye-bye, I'll be home soon,"
he said and left.
When I locked the door
the house seemed bigger.
Even curry rice
didn't taste good.
Father
you know
I hate it
when you go for three months.

Uriya Kei'ichi, fourth grade

ITCHO HANABUSA. *Bugaku Dances.* Early 18th century. Six-fold screen: color and gold leaf on paper, 72⅛ × 177⅝". The Metropolitan Museum of Art, New York; The Harry G. C. Packard Collection of Asian Art. Gift of Harry G. C. Packard and Purchase, Fletcher, Rogers, Harris Brisbane Dick and Louis V. Bell Funds, Joseph Pulitzer Bequest and The Annenberg Fund, Inc. Gift, 1975

My Hands

I folded a lot
of *origami*
and I'm tired but
my fingers are saying
"We want to fold!
We want to fold more!"

Itō Kozue, first grade

ORIGAMI. Paper ornaments on Christmas
tree. Courtesy of Japan Airlines

36

Tōrei Zenshi. *Ensō*. Mid-18th century. Ink on paper, 13 × 17¾". Private collection

Addition

One plus one
is two.
Mother plus father
is me.
Moon
plus stars
is sky.

Hoyano Emi, kindergarten

Headband

Today I used the abacus
and did lots of addition,
so my head got full of numbers inside
and it started to hurt really bad.
Grandma said
"When your head hurts,
you should put on a headband,"
and she tied one on me.
The pain went away
and the numbers also went away.

Naitō Yūki, second grade

The Ghost of Nine by Nine

The night after we started multiplication,
I had a dream.
The ghost of nine by nine was chasing me.
My mother was there.
"Help me!" I said, and she disappeared.
I had the feeling I was trapped
in a dark, dark world of nothingness—
it was that sort of dream.
"I won't be beat by multiplication," I said,
and went back to sleep. It was a scary dream.

Kobayashi Kazune, second grade

Kᴀᴍɪsᴀᴋᴀ Sᴇᴋᴋᴀ. *Path Through the Fields*. From *A World of Things*, vol. 3. 1910. Color woodblock print, 11⅛ × 17⅜″. Ravicz Collection

Rain Writing

Write the *kanji** for rain
and when you look at it,
you feel like outside a window
rain is falling.

Kobayashi Sōta, first grade

*Chinese character

Haiku

My mother
did the laundry
and I read a book.
I remembered two parts—
Ah, what silence this!
and
Early summer rain.
I was watching the weather
and suddenly
a *haiku* came:
"Again there is rain
falling and we're in trouble—
the laundry is out!"

Miyake Nobuhiro, first grade

Ogawa Hidehiko. Kanji for "rain". Ink
on paper

Brush Box

Why is a brush box
a brush box?
It's a box
that holds pencils.
But who
gave it this name?
It was probably
someone long ago.
Back then,
instead of pencils
it was brushes.
So it's a brush box
but now we use pencils
so to put pencils in it
must be okay.

Sekine Tomoaki, fourth grade

In the Postbox

In the postbox, the letters are talking.
"Where are you going?"
"I'm going here . . ."
and they show each other their backs.
"Oh, I see!"
they nod,
one by one asking everyone.

In the morning
they speak softly—
"goodbye . . ."
and they close their eyes.

Tashiro Maki, second grade

UNKNOWN. *Brush Box*. 18th–19th century. Black-and-gold lacquer box containing: a rectangular ink stone, a silver water pot, three brushes, a knife, and a stylet, 8¹³⁄₁₆ × 9¹¹⁄₁₆ × 1⅞". The Walters Art Gallery, Baltimore, Maryland

opposite:
TORII KIYONAGA. *Shigeyuki Executing Calligraphy*. 1783. Color woodcut print, 14¾ × 9⅝". Philadelphia Museum of Art. Given by Mrs. John D. Rockefeller

SOKUHI NYOICHI. *One-Line Writing*. Mid-17th century. Ink on paper, 49 × 12¼". Heinz Götze Collection, Heidelberg

Calligraphy

I put the brush on the paper.
Trying to go
cleverly
I pull the brush.
It's like it's being
chased by children.

Fujita Haruna, third grade

44

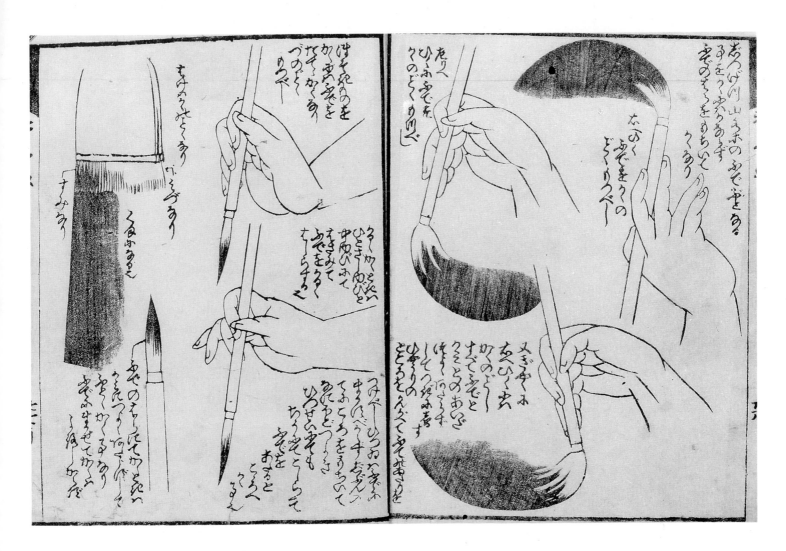

Katsushika Hokusai. *Drawing from*
Rijakuga Haya Oshiye, part 2. 1812.
Drawing. Courtesy, Museum of Fine Arts,
Boston. Gift of William Sturgis Bigelow

KATSUSHIKA HOKUSAI. *Turtles Under Water*. Edo period. Multicolored woodblock print, ōban. Tokyo National Museum

Woodblock Print

Shave the smooth face
make it look good—
it will show in the paper mirror.

Matsuda Takashi, fourth grade

46

Story

One day, I was a frog
and went to the river.
There was no frog
better than me.
In the river
there was a female frog.
She was beautiful.
We both fell in love
and we had
a wedding.
We never ever
got in fights.
We always
smiled.

Nakamura Isao, second grade

Frogs

Frogs are croaking
in the rice paddies.
When one stops
they all stop together
and when one starts,
together, they all start croaking again.
I wonder why they all start together?
I wonder why they all stop together?

Hosoda Ayumi, fourth grade

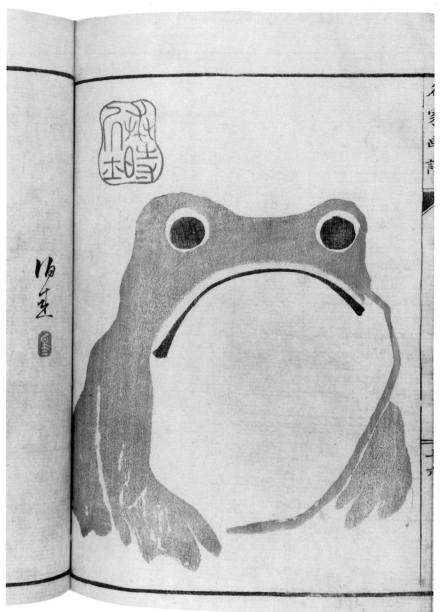

Matsumoto Hōji. *Toad*. From *A Book of Paintings by Celebrated Artists*. 1814. Woodblock print, 10⁹/₁₆ × 7⁵/₁₆" (page size). Ravicz Collection

Garbage Me

Garbage
garbage
garbage.
My friends are here—
everywhere.
The trash is taken.
Me too.
We go to the incinerator
and we burn.
And burn.
It's hot—
it's hot!
We turn to ashes.

Hirota Shōgo, first grade

YOKOO TADANORI. *Edo to Meiji.* 1986. Silkscreen on ceramic tile, 96 × 96". Designed for the exhibition "Tokyo: Form and Spirit," organized by Walker Art Center. Collection of the artist

Yoshida District

Yoshida district
is the place I live.
In the future
an expressway will come through here.
After they started
the construction work,
there were ruins
everywhere.
And lots
of burial mounds.
Yoshida district
is changing.
Day by day
we're losing
the green.

Takayama Hirofumi, fourth grade

Tosa Mitsuoki. *Cherry Blossoms with Poem Slips*. c. 1664–78. Six-fold screen: ink, colors, gold leaf, and powdered gold on silk, 56⅛ × 115½″. The Art Institute of Chicago; Kate S. Buckingham Collection

Cherry Blossoms Scatter

Scattering blossoms
one by one
with all their thoughts
they scatter
through people's hearts
they scatter
sadly they scatter
all of them
scatter.

Matsushima Yōko, sixth grade

51

Cherry Blossoms Laugh

The cherry blossom mother
laughs *o ho ho!*
The father laughs *ah ha ha!*
The blossom grandma laughs *hoo hoo hoo!*
and the grandpa *heh heh heh!*
The little blossom girl laughs *hee hee hee!*
and the boy goes *nyah nyah nyah!*
Lit by the streetlamps at night
the cherry blossom family is laughing, all together.
But when it rains, all together
they fall away and die.

Ōzeki Yukiko, second grade

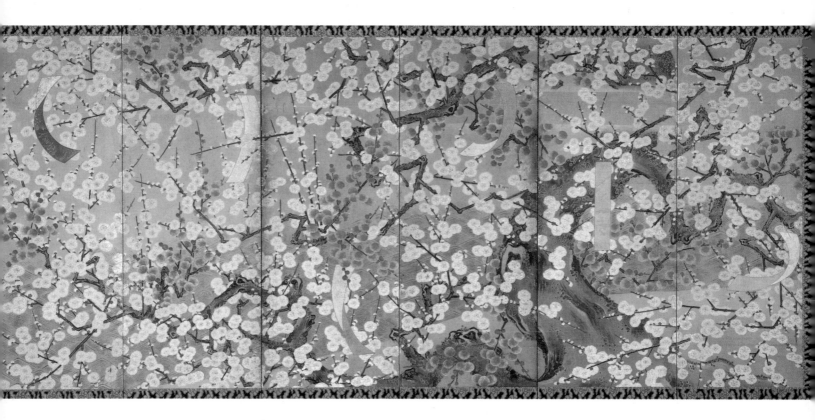

ANONYMOUS. *Red and White Blossoming Plum Trees*. n.d. Six-fold screen: color on paper, 60³/₈ × 136½". Los Angeles County Museum of Art. Etsuko and Joe Price Collection

Lull in the Plum Rains

The rain that fell until
yesterday stopped.
Careful of puddles
we play outside.
At last the sun
is laughing, but
the umbrella
is lonely.

Yokoyama Risa, sixth grade

Rain

From a sullen sky
rain, rain,
a gift from the gods
a few minutes' life
from above to below
without saying "hey"
without saying "ho"
pitter patter
falling lonely,
little drops in ones and twos
open a sure sadness
in my heart.

Kikuno Motoi, sixth grade

Rainlift

The rain lifted. The sun
glowed a little with evening colors
and I said hello to the sky.
The sky said "at last the rain has lifted,"
and—*ah ha ha*—gave a little laugh.
With that voice
all the crops in the field laughed.
And then
saying "please excuse me,"
the sun began to sink to the west.
It was evening, but still
from the sky far away
—*ah ha ha*—a laugh
came echoing.

Sawa Chihiro, third grade

ANDŌ HIROSHIGE. *Evening Rain on the Great Bridge*. From *One Hundred Views of Famous Places in Edo*. 1857. Woodblock print, ōban. Honolulu Academy of Arts. The James A. Michener Collection

Morning Glory Seed

I planted a seed.
It's like the moon.
It's like the moon
is speaking to me
through the seed's hole
and trying to teach me.

Iwagaki Takuya, second grade

Moss

Moss—
the gods thought
to give vanity to rocks
and it was made.

Takahashi Sayo, kindergarten

SHOKADO. *Fan-shaped Painting of Skein of Geese and Reflected Moon.* From *An Album of Shokado's Paintings.* 1804. Woodblock print, 12½ × 17⅝" (page size). Ravicz Collection

Sunset Sky

Mom—
the sunset sky is pretty, isn't it?
The crows are eating it.
Mmm, they say,
delicious!
But just
a little
bit sour.

Igarashi Yūko, kindergarten

Ogata Kōrin. *Iris and Bridge*. 18th century. Six-panel screen (one of a pair): paint and gold on paper, 70½ × 146¼". The Metropolitan Museum of Art, New York. Louisa E. McBurney Gift Fund, 1953

Rice Paddy Road

The Paddy Road is all-year pretty—
in spring it's flower pretty
in summer, grass pretty
in autumn it's pretty with bug noises
and in winter with snow,
our proud Paddy Road.
We walk to school on the Paddy Road.
We call it the Paddy Road because it's right in the middle
    of the rice paddies.
It's a name everyone thought of.

Sawada Mariko, third grade

Autumn

Grandma gave us
some *susuki* grass.
The *susuki*
stands straight
and serious
waiting for the moon.
When night comes,
there are bell-cricket noises
and slowly
it gets lonely.
Somehow,
I start to want
to turn the television on.

Yamada Daiji, second grade

Dewdrop

Today I saw a dewdrop,
a dewdrop perched neatly
on a blade of grass.
When you shake it the inside swirls,
shining in seven colors as it falls.
It's like a mother
pulling a lazy child by the hand.

Imai Kentarō, fourth grade

Weeds

Weeds have buds
weeds have leaves
weeds have flowers
and still weeds
are always left out,
though they're the same as flowers.
A long time ago
no one said "weeds"
and everyone was happy.

Aruga Shunsuke, third grade

above:

NAGASAWA ROSETSU. *Bamboo Grove*. 18th century. Ink on paper, mounted as a six-panel screen, 50¾ × 102¹³⁄₁₆". Worcester Art Museum, Worcester, Massachusetts. Eliza S. Paine Fund in memory of William R. and Frances T. C. Paine

left:

Kosode with Wild Ginger Against Mountain Lane and Mist. Middle Edo period. White satin with resist-dye and embroidery, 58⅝ × 24⅜". Kanebo Museum of Textiles, Osaka City

Bamboo Shoots

When I went to the bamboo grove out in back
there were bamboo shoots coming up all over.
Baby shoots laughing
mother shoots smiling
father shoots rustling—
they stretch and stretch
to see who is taller.
The bamboo family is full.

Watanabe Mina, third grade

Tosa Hirokane. *Ants Bearing Rice.* From *Amewakahikō-sōshi emaki—The Star Prince.* 15th century. Ink and colors on paper, 12¾ × 36⅛″ (overall). Museum für Ostasiatische Kunst, Staatliche Museen Preussischer Kulturbesitz, Berlin

If I Were an Ant

Suppose I
were an ant—
I'd be lazy
for sure.
And
I wouldn't save my food—
I'd eat lots.

Hitomi Takeshi, third grade

YAMASE MATSUTARO. *Cicada Kite*. From *The Art of the Japanese Kite* by Tal Streeter, Weatherhill Publishers, 1974

Wind

Today during music period
I was sitting by the window.
Outside a strong wind was blowing.
The schoolyard trees
were huddled in the wind, shivering.
It was entirely different
from the usual noisy courtyard.
The wind that came blowing
through the crack in the window
was something I've never felt until now.
It was such a wind that I wanted to stand
alone in the schoolyard.
I felt that the wind taught me
something even more important
than music study.

Shinohara Gō, fourth grade

Summer Mountaineers

When I look
at the cicadas
resting on a pine tree
they seem like mountaineers.
They climb, crying
jii jii!
then stopping a moment,
they seem to fall
and fly off to rest
in some other shade.

Tsukioka Kōsuke, third grade

Mount Fuji

It's tall.
It's very big.
When there's snow, it shines clean,
just between Yamanashi and Shizuoka.
At the top, the air is thin.
When you climb the mountain you feel good.
Everyone watches the peak.
A few hours time with Mount Fuji—
that's where I want to go—Mount Fuji,
the beautiful shining Mount Fuji.

Nagao Shin'ichi, fifth grade

Fir Tree

Struck by the sun
it won't turn.
Whipped by strong wind
it doesn't budge.
It spreads its branches
like Mount Fuji
and just stands still.
Stretching straight,
standing stiff,
in leaps and bounds
the fir tree grows.

Yamada Daiji, third grade

Automatic Ticket Machine

On a class trip to the train station,
they showed us the inside of the machine.
It's so
full of things
but it moves smoothly, humming,
and doesn't get stuck at all.
When you think it will hit something—
it moves smoothly, humming,
and doesn't hit anything.
When you think
it will get stuck—
it just slips
from place to place, humming.

It's incredible—
Japan is really moving ahead, isn't it?

Wada Mizuki, second grade

Kurobé Dam

Yesterday
it was the day after tomorrow,

today
it's tomorrow,

tomorrow
it will be today—

we're going to
Kurobé Dam!

Matsuzaki Yasuko, third grade

Railway Crossing

It's a railway crossing.
If you listen very carefully
the sound and the lamp
don't exactly match.
You can hear the gossip
of the old ladies nearby.
The people on a train
have many different looks.
If some are laughing,
then some are serious.
At the railway crossing,
you can't be bored.

Ushiyama Akinori, sixth grade

UNKNOWN. *First Electric Street Light on Tokyo's Ginza.* 1883. Woodblock print. Collection Ministry of Foreign Affairs, Tokyo

Big Buddha

Wow, it's big!
If you go close the face and eyes
and hands all get much bigger.
It was like being sucked up—
it was a very scary feeling.
I go even closer.
When I look up, there's a kind
face that seems to laugh a little,
and the eyes, too,
seem to be only slightly open.
The hands are linked before
the big body
and nodding head—
their shape becomes
a rugby ball.
Anyway, standing before
this big Buddha,
my feelings became
totally gentle feelings.

Kotado Yoriko, fifth grade

Offering

Grandpa,
if the Buddha
only ate the spirit of the rice cake,
then
can I eat the rest?

Kobayashi Wataru, first grade

Jocho. *Amida Nyorai.* 1053. Gilded
wood, 129⅞″ (height). Byodo-in, Uji

73

River

Since long, long ago
the river has been flowing.
At times it flows quietly
trickle trickle trickle
and at times noisy—
splash splash splash!
To me it seems just like
a human being.
The water runs high and gets furious,
the water runs low
and flows soft and weak,
and to me it seems just like
a human being.

Tonozaki Masaya, fourth grade

River's Secret

The cold
inside of the river
glitters and shines.
The surface is like glass.
The flow is distant.
Heave ho, heave ho . . .
it's almost like
there's a magnet there.
The river is the South Pole
and my feet are the North.
Heave ho, heave ho!
Ah, we're finally there—
the far shore.

Kuwajima Naoto, fourth grade

ANDŌ HIROSHIGE. *Kanaya: Ōi River and Distant Peaks.* From *The Fifty-Three Stations of the Tōkaidō.* 1834. Woodblock print, ōban. Honolulu Academy of Arts. The James A. Michener Collection

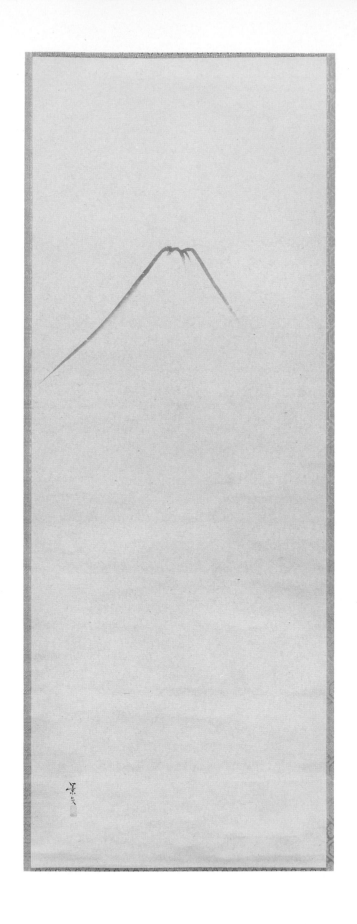

KEIBUN. *Fuji and Pine Trees* (a pair of kakemono). 19th century. Japanese ink and wash on paper, 44½ × 16¼″ each. The Minneapolis Institute of Arts. Bequest of Richard P. Gale

The Pool

The pool at summer's end
is green
and somehow sad.
It looks straight up at the sky
and the sky looks right back down.
Together they stare
facing each other
waiting for winter—
the pool and the sky.

Aoki Kazutoshi, third grade

River Sound

Together grandma and I
got out of the bath.
I was hot,
so I turned on the fan.
"This is a real luxury,"
grandma said.
"A long time ago
when we left the bath
we'd sit on a bench outside
and cool off slowly,"
she explained.
I took grandma's hand
and we went outside.
It's true—up on the bridge, listening
to the sound of the river flowing,
even my feelings
got cool.

Sasaki Shō, fourth grade

OGURA RYŪSON. *Yaomatsu Restaurant at Mukojima.* 1881. Woodblock print, 8¹³⁄₁₆ × 13¼". Machida City Museum of Graphic Arts

Cycling

I rode straight along
the banks of the Edogawa,
and saw
about a hundred carp
swimming upstream.
My bicycle went
ryuryuryuryuryuryuryu—
it was saying
"No matter how I run,
my legs are still strong."

Yasuno Ken, first grade

Crayfish

Crayfish
have scissors.
I caught one
and it snapped the scissors at me—
snip snip—
it was angry.
It curled its tail
and swung it down behind.
I wonder which is stronger,
a crab or a crayfish?
A crayfish with no claws
would be interesting.
It would look like a *samurai*.

Yokoi Katsunori, second grade

KATSUKAWA SHUNSHO. *Karigane, Five Men*. c. 1780. One of five woodblock prints, $12 \times 15\frac{1}{2}$". The Nelson-Atkins Museum of Art, Kansas City, Missouri; Nelson Fund

UNKNOWN. *Manuscript Box* (top). 19th century. Lacquer, 2¾ × 13⅝ × 6″. The Metropolitan Museum of Art, New York; Bequest of Benjamin Altman, 1913

White Crest Butterfly

Yesterday
I found
a white crest butterfly.
It was dead.
My fingers where I pinched the wings
turned all white.
Maybe all the memories
of this butterfly's life
turn to white powder in its wings.

Hirano Yōko, second grade

The Sad Butterfly

Though he worked so hard to leave the cocoon
he never stretched his wings,
he died before he got outside,
he became food for the baby cocoon wasps,
and it's very sad.
He was a tiny and round
and very cute caterpillar.
Though he worked so hard to become a
cocoon,
what troubles there are
in the butterfly world
is something people can't understand.

Kobayashi Chiharu, fourth grade

Cockroach

It's always naughty
and everyone
says they don't like it,
but a cockroach
really
wants to be
a butterfly.
A cockroach
really
is much sadder
than we think.

Minagawa Kaoru, kindergarten

The Chrysalis Dance

Our class
is keeping
a caterpillar.
If you look steadily
at the chrysalis
it shakes its bottom,
just
as if it were dancing.
The chrysalis dance
would be pretty bad
if a person did it.
But
for a chrysalis it was very good.

Matsumoto Kōta, fourth grade

Carp Kite

When a little wind blows
it swims happily.
When a strong wind blows
it swims shivering, unhappy.
When the carp kite is unhappy
I am too.
When there is no wind
the carp kite sleeps—standing up.

Hirai Toshie, fifth grade

SUZUKI HARUNOBU. *A Parody of the Immortal Chi'in-kao*. Mid-18th century. Woodblock print. Collection Mrs. Irma Grabhorn

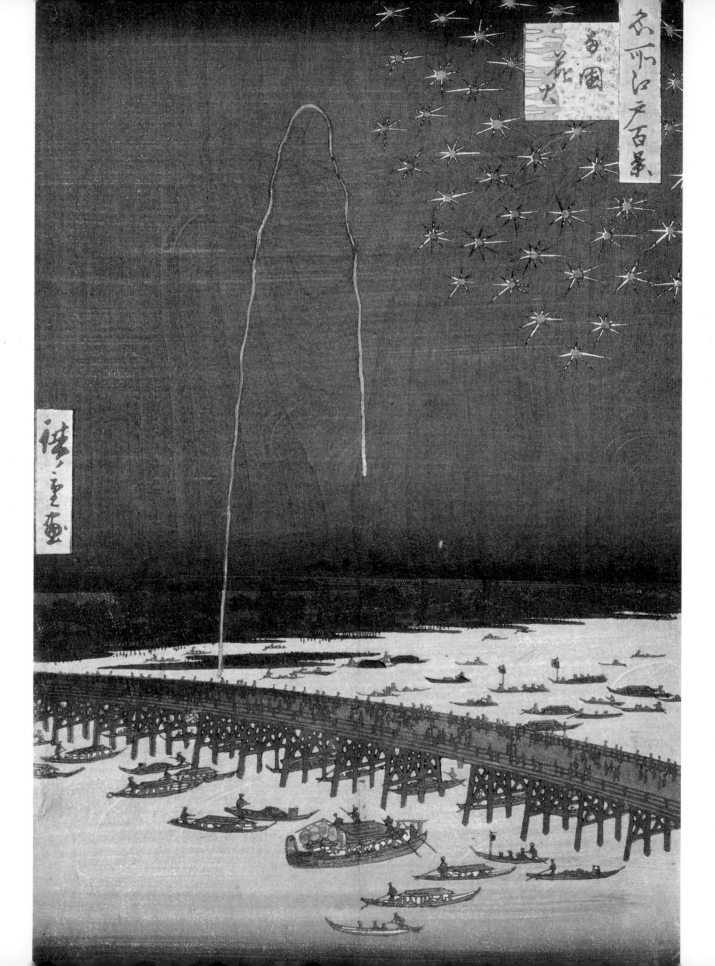

The Sky Is Busy

The lighthouse
on that island
is shining.
Helicopters in the sky
are shining.
Boats are glittering, too.
And with a bang
someone is shooting off fireworks.
Today the sky
is very busy.

Ishikawa Megumi, kindergarten

Fireworks

The fireworks
are more beautiful
than my mother.
But
they're lonely.

Hizuka Shino, kindergarten

ANDŌ HIROSHIGE. *Fireworks at Ryogoku Bridge*. From *One Hundred Views of Famous Places in Edo*. 1858. Woodblock print, ōban. Honolulu Academy of Arts. The James A. Michener Collection

Tears

When I cry
there is a festival in my heart.
There are lots of drums
and the gods are beating them hard—
it echoes inside me
and the tears roll out.

Matsumoto Kanako, fourth grade

The Bonito Dance

I sprinkled bonito fish
into hot noodles
and it was wonderful!
The bonito danced.
The thin shaved bodies
twisted and turned,
they danced like they were alive.
Together with the bonito
I twisted and turned and danced.

Shirai Fumiya, first grade

HOGEN TANSHIN. *The Hosai Nembutsu Dance (Rice Harvest Festival Dance)*. c. 1715. Woodblock print, 15⅛ × 10½″. The Art Institute of Chicago. Frederick W. Gookin Collection

Fireflies

ELISHŌSAI CHŌKI. *Firefly Hunt*. Mid-1790s. Woodblock print, 10⅛ × 15⅛". Collection Mrs. Irma Grabhorn

In the rice paddy rushes
there are flashing lights.
Those lights
are a gift of the moonlight—
a long, long time before a long time ago
when the moon began to shine
it spilled some light by mistake
and said "Oh!"
and there were fireflies.

Takahashi Chiharu, fourth grade

Sparks

We had a
campfire.
Sparks of fire rising out of the kindling
just
like *ayu* fish swimming.
And then, sparks
falling down from above
just like fireflies.

Sakuma Chie, fifth grade

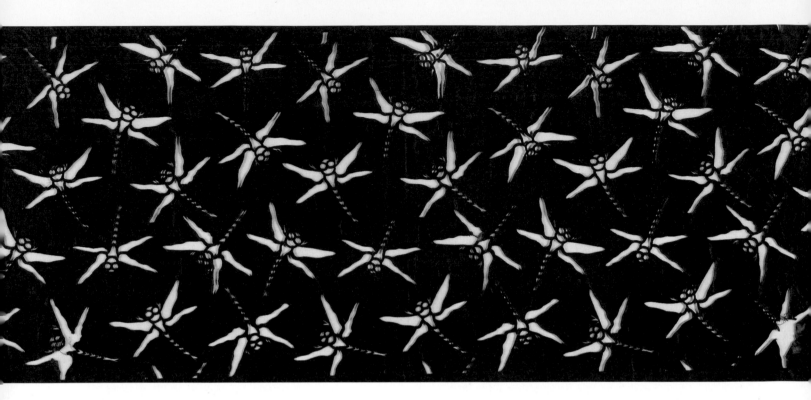

UNKNOWN. *Dragonflies* (stencil). Edo
period, late 19th century. Paper and silk
thread, 9½ × 16″. The Art Institute of
Chicago. Frederick W. Gookin Collection

Goodbye

"It's already fall, isn't it?"
said mother, and I said
"Yes it is."
Next to us, the bell-cricket said
"Yes, it is."
The sheep-cloud in the sky agreed,
"Yes, it is!"
The sunflower
a little sadly said
"goodbye."

Yamada Daiji, fourth grade

Red Dragonfly

Red face
red clothes
face dyed red
in the evening sun
as if it got drunk
from too much *saké*
flying happily across
the red-dyed sky
just like it's swimming
wings spread wide
cheerful in red
for today's good party
living
its short life
with all its heart.

Yamada Kyōko, fifth grade

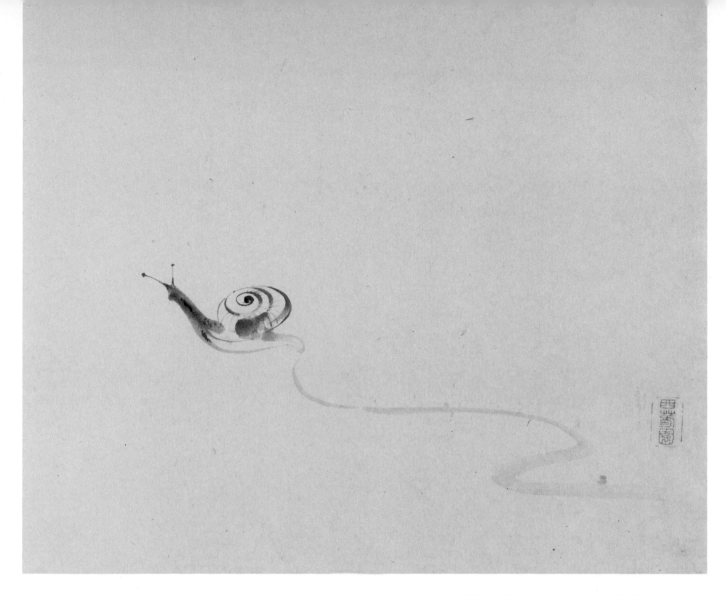

HŌEN. *Snail*. c. 1840. Ink and light colors on paper, 10⅝ × 12⁹⁄₁₆″. Copyright The British Museum

Snail Watching

A snail
runs *choko choko*
slowly away—
please allow him
the time
to be gone.

Arashida Rie, kindergarten

Snail

Rolling round
and round
the typhoon
made the snail.

Iwazaki Yasuhiro, kindergarten

Maple Leaf

The bright red maple leaves
flutter falling
down to the ground.
I picked one up
and took it in my hand.
"Aren't you pretty,"
I said
and the red color seemed
to get a little darker.
It was embarrassed.

Akisato Yumi, third grade

Suzuki Kiitsu. *Fresh Paulownia/Maple Leaves*. n.d. Pair of hanging scrolls: ink and color on silk, 47 × 14″ each. Los Angeles County Museum of Art. Etsuko and Joe Price Collection

SAKAI HOITSU (1761–1828). *Sweeping Maple Leaves*. n.d. Hanging scroll: ink and light colors on paper, 43½ × 18⁵⁄₁₆″. Los Angeles County Museum of Art. Etsuko and Joe Price Collection

Leaf Journey

Leaves
make an incredible voyage.
From seed to sprout
they turn into trees
and then fall in the river
and float away,
just like that
they turn into soil.
Leaves make themselves
full of memories.
I think
they must be satisfied.

Tezuka Misako, second grade

Persimmon

A very
sweet persimmon.
Persimmon color
fits with
the blue in the sky—
the persimmon color
is the sunset.
Look at it carefully
and it's laughing.
How cute!

Sakamoto Sachiko, second grade

Crow

A crow is pitch black.
You can't see where its eyes are.
A big one looks like
a flying *sushi* roll.
A very big one looks like
a flying garbage bag.

Aoki Suguru, third grade

UNKNOWN. *Moon Scene with Crow.*
c. 1770. Paint on paper, 75 × 16⅞".
Alsdorf Collection, Chicago

Crane

There's a crane.
It looks very cold.

"Why
don't you go somewhere warm?"
I want to ask.

But
it wouldn't understand.

Still
I really want to ask.

Oda Shinobu, third grade

Itō Jakuchū. *Pine, Plum and Crane.*
Early 1760s. Hanging scroll: ink and
light colors on paper, 53⅞ × 24". Tokyo
National Museum

The Day the Typhoon Comes

The day the typhoon comes
heavy looking clouds
put on an ugly face
and go moving.
It's because a magic child
is riding them.
The magic child
is looking somewhere far away
and steering the clouds in that direction.
The clouds seem angry
but they move anyway.
Even so many clouds
can't beat a magic child.

Fukushima Yūko, sixth grade

Discrimination and Teasing

At times in class
there is a child
with a lot of followers.
And then against him,
always weakly,
there is a child
being teased.
The people around
just laugh and watch
and hardly anybody
tries to stop it.
Is this discrimination and teasing
something nobody can get off their hands?

Satō Rina, sixth grade

UNKNOWN. *Thunder God.* 13th century. Wood, with lacquer, gold leaf, paint, and inlaid eyes, 39⅜" (height from base of left knee). Sanjūsangendō, Kyoto

Fifth Grade

From today on, I'm in fifth grade! My chest felt tight as I took the road to school. It felt like I was taking that road for the first time. Fourth grade seemed like a dream to me. When I got to school everything was quiet and when I came to the classroom suddenly everyone was looking at me. I felt like a transfer student. I was all shy. But I steeled my shoulders and entered the classroom. In my heart I was shouting, "I *am* a part of this class!" Everybody seemed much taller. I thought I had gotten smaller. I was a little embarrassed. But at that moment a fifth grade wind began to blow.

Endō Mina, fifth grade

The Sea

It rained and rained and rained.
Little baby rivers went flowing
away into a big, big pool.
The river babies
asked the big pool
"What in the world are you?"
The big pool answered—
"I am the Sea!"

Inoue Yashiro, second grade

Lonely Night

Crashhh . . .
on a lonely night with nobody there
I listen to the ocean
and somehow feel like
it's telling me a story.
Somehow
listening to the sea sounds
relaxes my heart.
My sadness
disappears somewhere.
I become quiet inside.
My sadness
melts into the sea.

Kida Yasuhiro, fifth grade

YOICHIRO HIRASE. *A Group of Shells.*
1915. Woodblock print, 9¾ × 14⅛″.
Ravicz Collection

Shell

Jingle jingle jingle—
a shell is taken by someone.
O kind
mother sea
goodbye,
goodbye.

Koi Tomoko, sixth grade

Snow

Snow on the trees likes the morning sun,
the gold glittering
illumination.
Snow in the deep mountains likes
storytelling—*chatter chatter,*
talking with the sun.
Snow in the road seems ticklish,
gets trampled with a
squish squish, laughing.
Snow on the roof relaxes,
gets a perfect score for its heavy nap.
Snow at nighttime loves vanity,
strolling with the diamond-studded moon.

Kikuno Motoi, sixth grade

IKENO TAIGA. *Tree Forms*. From
The Drawing Book of Taiga. 1804.
Woodblock print, 11¾ × 15¹⁄₁₆″ (page
size). Ravicz Collection

Footprints

Red boots walk
on snow
trampled by nobody.

Then
looking back
only footprints
remained.
Though nobody was there
only footprints
remained
going
on and on.

Doi Yōko, fifth grade

New Moon

The sun
is slipping
behind the hill.
It takes a bath
and eats dinner
and goes to sleep.
The new moon
stayed too long
in the bath
and finally melted.

Katagiri Eriko, kindergarten

Amazing Place

This year in the summer we went to Matsushima.
When we came to the shrine
a world I had already seen lay before me.
It was the first time I went—but it was amazing.
I got a little bit scared.
No matter how much I thought or asked anyone
it was definitely the first time I had come.
I thought that I must have come here
in a previous life.
I wanted to know what animal I was in that life.

Kakimoto Kentarō, fifth grade

New Year's Day

The sun got up early
in a clear blue sky
the morning of that day
and waited for us.
There was a long line
waiting for a turn
at the shrine by the sea.
Everyone went walking
to clean out their hearts
for the New Year.

Okami Chiho, second grade

ATTRIBUTED TO NONOMURA SŌTATSU.
Scene from the Ise Monogatari: Beach at Sumiyoshi. Edo period, early 17th century. Album leaf: color and gold on paper, 9⅝ × 8¼″. The Cleveland Museum of Art. John L. Severance Fund

Godzilla

Godzilla
blows fire
from his mouth—
he's got toothaches
for sure.

Ono Hiromu, kindergarten

Maruyama Ōshin. *Dragon Emerging from the Sea*. n.d. Hanging scroll: ink on silk, 11 15/16 × 5 15/16". Los Angeles County Museum of Art. Etsuko and Joe Price Collection

Scary Things

What scares me
is a ghost.
A ghost screaming
in the pitch dark.
But there's something
scarier than that.
It's war.
Hundreds and thousands of people
in an atomic explosion
were killed
and there was
a sea of blood,
an earth of blood.
Hiroshima especially
seems cruel and sad.
That time America
was the devil.
Didn't they think
it was sad?

Kobayashi Hideki, second grade

War and Peace

War is a fearful thing
that snatches away people's lives,
that changes their hearts.
Peace is a thing that makes everyone happy,
that everyone hopes for,
that clears people's hearts.
War and peace—everyone wants peace
but these things called *people*
are greedy creatures—
give them peace and they'll turn it to war.
People are a fearful thing.

Fujita Ryō, seventh grade

YOSHITOSHI. *Torments of Hell: Death of Tairo Kiyomori*. 1884. Polychrome woodblock print, 9¼ × 14″ (each panel of triptych). Collection Walton Rawls, New York

Baseball with Muscle

Plop! The muscle on my arm
fell out. When I looked down,
it was round like a ball so I played baseball with it.
The muscle flew pretty far.
When in surprise I looked at my arm
there was a crack there.
With a start I opened my eyes—
it was a dream.
I moved my arm carefully
and it was just as usual.
When we got up in the morning
I told my mother
the whole story
and somehow
the strange, uneasy feeling
disappeared.

Igarashi Daiki, first grade

Goggled clay figure (found at Fujikabu
site, Akita Pref.). Jōmon period. Clay, 8½"
high. Laboratory of Archeology, Tōhoku
University, Japan

Dream Country

Up above the sky
there is a dream country.
There
lots and lots of cars
and steam engines are running.
They carry dreams.
There is also
a locomotive.
And there
nothing but sunny days will do.
In the dream country
children without dreams
visit a robot
called "Dreamseller"
and receive
many different dreams.

Naitō Maiko, fifth grade

Alien Fishing

Aliens catch humans
humans catch fish
fish eat plankton
and plankton
eat dead fish bodies—
fish eat plankton
humans catch fish
and to catch humans
aliens go fishing
with money on their poles.

Miyoshi Hiromichi, third grade

ITŌ JAKUCHŪ. *Mandarin Ducks and Snow Covered Reeds*. 17th–18th century. Hanging scroll: ink and color on silk. Los Angeles County Museum of Art. Etsuko and Joe Price Collection

World Without Sound

Shhh . . .
a silent world.
Even if you try to talk
you can't.
You can't telephone either.
You live just thinking
by yourself.
Ears
are just part of the body.
Around us
are any number of people, but—
we're all alone.

Hayashi Chisato, sixth grade

ACKNOWLEDGMENTS

WORKING ON this collection was an utterly thrilling prospect from the start, but the project was accomplished with an ease and pleasure that I would never have imagined and which I owe to many people. At the top of the list is Paul Gottlieb at Abrams, who is largely responsible for this being a book instead of a series of jottings in a spiral-bound travel diary; Ellen Rosefsky, Darilyn Lowe Carnes, and Neil Hoos made it the book that it is. In Japan, Nihei Yoshiko provided unflagging assistance as well as crucial feedback on the translations. The time that I spent abroad was made possible with funding from the Japanese Ministry of Education. The illustrations were gathered largely due to the good graces of Professor John Rosenfield and the librarians at the Rubell Library, Sackler Museum, Cambridge, Mass. Also, I would like to offer special thanks to Professor Edwin A. Cranston; to Amika, Yasushi, and Ikehara Tomoko; to my sisters, Miri and Jenny; and to Annie Leonard, all of whom provided invaluable lessons on translation, on poetry, and on life. Finally, let this anthology end where it began—with an appreciation of the brilliant, funny kids who wrote these poems, and of their Japanese champion, Kawasaki Hiroshi.

B. N.

INDEX OF POEMS

Photograph Credits

Photograph (c) 1993, The Art Institute of Chicago. All Rights Reserved: title page (Christopher Gallagher), pp. 7, 13, 50-51 (Robert Hashomoto), 89, 92, endpapers; Joan Lebold Cohen: p. 72; Tibor Franyo: pp. 54, 68; Ingeborg Klinger: p. 44; Jurgen Liepe: pp. 62-63; Sakamoto: pp. 78, 117; Tal Streeter: pp. 21, 64, 108; L. Sully-Jaulmes: jacket front, p. 29; Richard Todd: p. 47; Tokyo National Museum: pp. 12, 17, 20, 46, 99, 101; A. J. Wyatt: p. 43.